RESTORING NOTRE-DAME DE PARIS

Rebirth of the Legendary Gothic Cathedral

The photographs featured in this book were produced as part of a partnership between the public body responsible for the conservation and restoration of Notre-Dame Cathedral in Paris and Magnum Photos.

Other Schiffer books on related subjects
Cathedrals Built by the Masons, Russell Herner, 978-0-7643-4840-2
Monumental: The Greatest Architecture Created by Humankind, Kunth Verlag, 978-0-7643-6418-1
Stone in Traditional Architecture, David Campbell, 978-0-7643-3614-0

Originally published as *Notre-Dame: Histoire d'une renaissance* by Bayard Editions, Montrouge Cedex, France © 2021 Bayard Editions
Translated from the French by Rebecca DeWald

Library of Congress Control Number: 2023941091

Type set in Cheswick/Monion/ DIN

ISBN: 978-0-7643-6727-4
Printed in China

Published by Schiffer Publishing, Ltd.
4880 Lower Valley Road
Atglen, PA 19310
Phone: (610) 593-1777; Fax: (610) 593-2002
Email: Info@schifferbooks.com
Web: www.schifferbooks.com

For our complete selection of fine books on this and related subjects, please visit our website at www.schifferbooks.com. You may also write for a free catalog.

Schiffer Publishing's titles are available at special discounts for bulk purchases for sales promotions or premiums. Special editions, including personalized covers, corporate imprints, and excerpts, can be created in large quantities for special needs. For more information, contact the publisher.

We are always looking for people to write books on new and related subjects. If you have an idea for a book, please contact us at proposals@schifferbooks.com.

PHOTOGRAPHS AND TEXT BY

PATRICK ZACHMANN

WITH OLIVIER DE CHÂLUS
FOREWORD BY GENERAL JEAN-LOUIS GEORGELIN

RESTORING NOTRE-DAME DE PARIS

Rebirth of the Legendary Gothic Cathedral

SCHIFFER PUBLISHING

4880 Lower Valley Road · Atglen, PA 19310

Contents

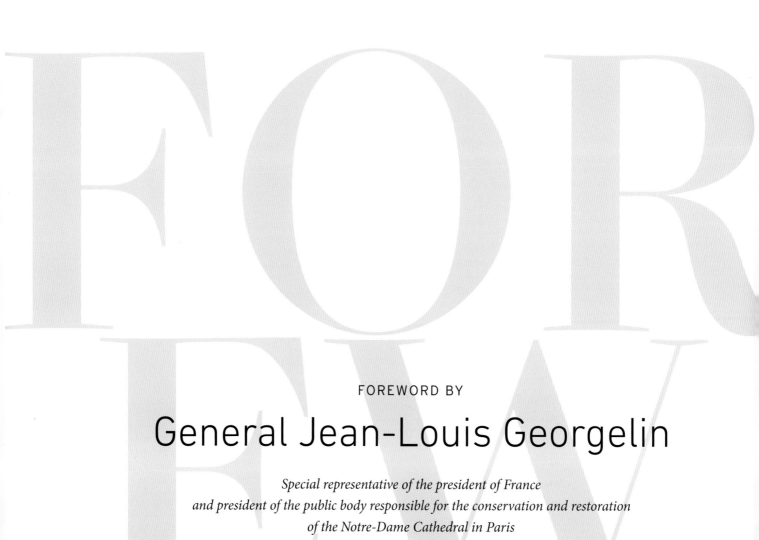

General Jean-Louis Georgelin

*Special representative of the president of France
and president of the public body responsible for the conservation and restoration
of the Notre-Dame Cathedral in Paris*

The first photograph of Notre-Dame de Paris is probably a daguerreotype from the mid-nineteenth century, which must have taken Louis Daguerre, the inventor of this still-new technology, entailing hours of preparation and setup.

Since then, the cathedral has become a popular motif for millions of visitors and is one of the most photographed historic buildings in Europe and probably worldwide.

Now, the building site of Notre-Dame and the craftspeople who tirelessly work there are uncovered by the passionate and singular gaze of photographer Patrick Zachmann from Magnum Photos.

This extraordinary human adventure, in the service of a historic building whose destiny exceeds ours, deserved to be documented and passed on to posterity. Thus, from the beginning of the construction work to secure the cathedral, it was very important to me that this talented photographer could visit the site regularly to show admirers of Notre-Dame the precise movements with which these craftspeople work, these people who are genuine experts in the field of cathedrals.

In emphasizing the spectacular operations that allowed us to save Notre-Dame, Patrick's work on the site to secure the cathedral is a homage to all those who see to its recovery and strive to restore it to its former splendor. Beauty is the catalyst of the cathedral's rebirth, and these photographs by Patrick are a testament to that. They reveal to us as much the beauty of Notre-Dame's Gothic architecture as they show the energy, know-how, and pride of these craftspeople.

Prologue
April 2019

Monday, April 15, 2019, 7:30 p.m. I am standing in front of Notre-Dame, alongside some tourists and Parisians in shock about what is happening before our eyes: the cathedral is on fire. Some people cry, and all are upset about this traumatic spectacle.

How far will this fire spread? The jets from the fire hoses seem so pathetic in the face of the burgeoning flames. I head toward the Quai d'Orléans, where people are standing shoulder to shoulder, filming with their cell phones. Everyone is aware that this is a historic moment.

The Rift

June 2019

Tuesday, June 25, 2019. I can finally enter the cathedral. Since the fire, I have not stopped thinking about this moment: I desperately wanted to see the damage inside caused by this disaster that had afflicted this heritage site. On my first visit, I am accompanied by Didier Durand, who runs the stone-masonry company that was undertaking work when the fire broke out, and by two employees of the communications department of the French Ministry of Culture.

Countless bits of debris, stones, fragments of charred beams, and scrap metal are littering the floor of the nave. Through a gaping hole above, caused by the collapse of the 315-foot-tall (96 meter) spire, you can see a section of the sky and some scaffolding. One image strikes me: that of the chairs left in place, which lets you imagine the worshipers who were here shortly before the fire broke out. The scene is upsetting. There is one sole consolation, however: miraculously, nobody was hurt.

The nave of Notre-Dame de Paris and, in the background, the high altar dating from the nineteenth century, which was partially destroyed, but its cross remained intact.

I went to visit a couple of residents of the nearby Île Saint-Louis in the Seine. Denise and Claude have just celebrated their sixtieth wedding anniversary. They live at the Quai aux Fleurs behind the cathedral, and just in front of the spot where I always park my scooter to visit the worksite. They are very friendly and warm people, and both are members of the Association for the Protection of the Site of Notre-Dame and Its Surrounding Area. They tell me that on the evening of April 15, journalists and television crews marched in and out of their apartment, and some even stayed until 4:00 in the morning.

I ask Denise to tell me about the fire: "On April 15, we were just coming home from doing our grocery shopping. The phone rang. It was 6:45 p.m. I picked up. It was a friend from the association who lives on Rue Chanoinesse, and she said to me, 'The cathedral is on fire!' My husband and I rushed to the balcony, where we did indeed see the first flames. The base of the spire was white hot.

"The firefighters arrived late," she continues, "because the Pont de l'Archevêché across the Seine was blocked. They came via Sévigné Street and Cardinal-Lemoine Street. They had a 98-foot-long (30 meter) ladder and short water hoses. It seemed ridiculous. I shouted from the balcony: 'Why such short hoses? Why not take the water from the Seine?' The reinforcements arrived from the Louvre, with a ladder 295 feet (90 meters) tall and a system that allowed them to pump water straight from the Seine, but they arrived only twenty minutes later. The firefighters were heroic. They understood that the roof would collapse but that the towers needed to be saved.

"The heat on the balcony was unbearable. If the bells had dropped, the cathedral would have been destroyed. It was apocalyptical, like in a horror movie . . . journalists and TV teams were on our balcony. There was such turmoil. It was not until the next day that I truly realized what had happened, and tears came to my eyes. The spire was gone. I hadn't had a bad dream. I was distraught."

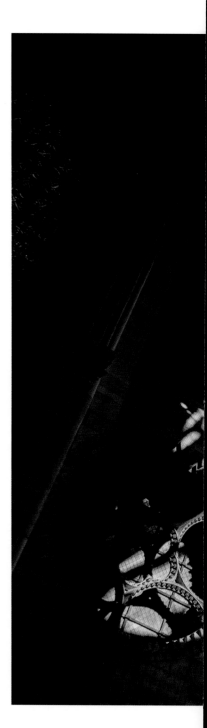

"I felt a fascination for this fire," Claude continues, "and at the same time, terror. And at one point, while the fire was still raging, we heard bells ringing. What left most of an impression on me was the heat and the noise. The spire came down with an incredibly loud crash."

Claude continues his account: "At first, when I saw the cathedral in flames, I thought to myself: it's nothing. I simply couldn't fathom the cathedral burning down. Later, I understood. We saw firefighters ascend the staircase of the north rose window. They looked tiny in comparison with the huge flames. We could hear the creaking of the roof truss. From the balcony, you could see flames across the rose window.

"And the most troubling thing of all was that it happened during Holy Week," he continues.

"We have never been blasé about the benevolent, almost human presence of Notre-Dame. It has been part of our daily lives. A universally shared feeling. For believers, it is a building of major importance; for others, a marvel of Gothic architecture, with admirable works of art. The most beautiful thing humankind has created."

And Denise finishes off this thought: "All those hands that built this historic building with the means available at the time, that's what moves me."

"The fire spread toward the towers at an incredible speed," Claude tells me. "It burned all night. At 4:30 a.m., it was pretty much under control."

Then they discovered this heap of scrap metal, of charred beams. A vision of immense sadness. The scaffolding withstood 2,730 degrees Fahrenheit (1,500° Celsius). The fire gave off a heat of 1,740 degrees Fahrenheit (950° Celsius) in some places. Now it's like a giant pick-up-sticks game. If you touch one tube, the whole thing might come tumbling down."

About 200 tons of scaffolding above the transept crossing were welded by the flames, and hundreds of scorched beams remain on top of the arches of the vaulted ceiling, where they form a huge tangled mess that needs to be removed.

A VIEW FROM HISTORY BY OLIVIER DE CHÂLUS

Notre-Dame de Paris on Fire

Before 2019, the history of the Parisian cathedral had featured four fires. The first, in 1218, was caused by an English thief who had sneaked into the choir loft and set fire to the curtains when trying to steal the lit candlesticks from the high altar. Although the medieval chronicles make mention of this event, it had limited consequences. Nine hundred silver marks were spent on replacing the silk drapes turned to ashes by the flames. The sum was certainly considerable, but the reported material damage remained contained.

The next and probably the most famous fire occurred only in the words of Victor Hugo. We pick up the story in 1480. The cathedral is under attack in the middle of the night, and a huge crowd has thronged to the cathedral square, preparing to break down the church doors, strip the house of worship of its treasures, and kidnap Esmeralda. To defend her, Quasimodo makes use of the ongoing construction works on the roof truss and piles up some roofing material to form a huge pyre on the flat roof above the façade between the two towers, setting it alight. Channeled toward the gargoyles, "two streams of molten lead were pouring from the top of the building upon the thickest part of the crowd," writes the author of *The Hunchback of Notre-Dame de Paris* (translated by Henry L. Williams). "This sea of men had subsided beneath the boiling metal, which had made, at the two points where it fell, two black and smoking holes

in the rabble, such as hot water would make in a snowdrift."

But this rain of boiling metal is not enough to effectively disperse the assailants, whose "rage found ladders and multiplied the torches; and, in a few moments, Quasimodo beheld with consternation a fearful rabble mounting on all sides to the assault of Notre-Dame."

A few pages later, Esmeralda is freed. This inferno constitutes the culmination of this monument of a novel published in 1831. Featured in its various audiovisual adaptations, this fire has also become the subject of numerous illustrations since the first publication of *The Hunchback of Notre-Dame*, one of the most important works of nineteenth-century literature.

The next fire featured in a work that equally marked its and subsequent centuries, the well-known *Dictionnaire de l'architecture médiévale* (*Dictionary of Medieval Architecture*) by the architect Eugène Viollet-le-Duc. He describes the fire in the section "Cathedral" in the second volume, published in 1843. It is the eve before the famous restoration works begin, which are at the heart of Viollet-le-Duc's monumental undertaking to write the first study of medieval buildings. The architect had observed that the flying buttresses and roof truss of Notre-Dame dated from after the second quarter of the thirteenth century, unlike the main structure of the Parisian cathedral, which had been built seventy years earlier.

He therefore sought to explain this anachronism, which he assumed to be the result of modifications made to the cathedral. As a means of justifying these, he invented a fire, which he dated to around 1230–40, "of which," he writes, "history makes no mention, but whose traces are visible in the monument." The flames apparently ravaged through the upper parts, burned down the roofs, and demolished the building's buttressing to the point that it had to be rebuilt in its entirety.

It was indeed the perfect justification. It was probably also the perfect hypothesis in the spirit of the nineteenth-century search for the Romanesque. However, the building has not retained any of the traces that Viollet-le-Duc said he spotted. Considering the damage caused by the 2019 fire, the marks left by the flames Viollet-le-Duc evoked would have been so numerous that several of them would certainly still be visible. Conversely, neither the 2019 inferno nor any other fire caused damage to the extent described in the *Dictionnaire*. For these reasons, researchers in the early twentieth century began to refute the historical accuracy of this event, while acknowledging the basis of Viollet-le-Duc's reflections: the idea that the cathedral must have undergone major modifications in the thirteenth century. These transformations remain difficult to explain today unless one were to postulate the hypothesis that the construction work had progressed much more slowly than has been assumed until now, and that these were not modifications but the result of the normal course of the works.

Finally, an aborted arson attempt before dawn on May 24, 1871, threatened the cathedral to share the fate of so many other Parisian monuments destroyed during the days of the Paris Commune, which history would subsequently remember as the "Semaine sanglante": the bloody week. The Communards' attacks against the Catholic Church had reached their peak: early that morning, Georges Darboy, archbishop of Paris, was shot. Fifteen Communards broke into the cathedral, piled up furniture in the transept, at the foot of the altar, and in the nave, and formed three fire heaps that they set alight with petroleum. We owe the suppression of the flames that had already reached the height of the organ case in the nave to the valiant courage of the medical staff at the nearby Hôtel-Dieu, who feared that the fire could spread to their hospital. But researchers only recently discovered that this fire, albeit oft repeated in the historiography of the cathedral, had been lit by the press; that is, it was the sole invention of the propaganda machine against the Communards. This fire was only ever lit in ink.

The fire of Victor Hugo's novel, which broke out while roofing works were underway, inevitably seems prophetic. We recognize in these pages the firefighters battling against the flames, the tactics of the plan to safeguard the artworks on the evening of the fire and in the days that followed, the lead that kept driving away the Parisians and crowds of tourists from the heart of the Île de la Cité. The works and hypotheses posited by Viollet-le-Duc naturally remind us of the uncertainties with which current research of the site is faced. How could one then not see in this bruised symbol, the image of which the media have shared the world over, the attack on the French nation's cathedral as recounted in the nineteenth-century press?

Apart from a few silk fabrics, these four fires had not caused any damage. On the contrary, through their narratives—whether they be literary, academic, political, or in the media—these "fires" helped shape a popular and scholarly image that made the 2019 fire what it was, beyond the damage it caused. To become aware of its meaning, just imagine for a moment what a fire similar to that of 2019 would have done to another building comparable to Notre-Dame de Paris. Notre-Dame de Paris is larger and much more alive than its material presence alone, and to gain a full measure of it we must delve deeper into the strange relationship that this place has been able to build with the people.

Saving the Ruins
July–December 2019

Tuesday, July 2, 2019. I have always felt the urge to project myself into the stories of others through the reverberations they evoke in me. As for Notre-Dame de Paris, I would never have engaged in this subject if I had not experienced these moments of intense emotion on April 15, alongside many other Parisians and tourists.

I have always used the medium of photography to tell the story of anonymous people in the web of a larger historical context.

Rope access technicians are installing various nets in the cathedral to catch falling debris that could damage other parts and injure the craftspeople.

At Notre-Dame, I meet archeologists who conscientiously note down every single trace of this memory written in stone, wood, and other materials. Their analyses will allow architects to reassemble the destroyed sections, like a huge puzzle.

From the vanished spire to the gaping hole in the place where the roof once was: How will it all be reborn?

To prevent stones from falling, the debris is collected by robots before being sorted by specialists, many of whom work in the police forensics department.

The most-skilled craftspeople working in various trades have joined forces to meet the challenge of restoring this national monument. I feel the genuine enthusiasm and tremendous energy of the journey people and craftspeople, and the architects and researchers I meet. They all are aware that they are part of an extraordinary collective adventure. Me included.

Before the restoration can begin, the priority is to secure the historic building to avoid further collapse. It is particularly necessary in order to save and sort the remains.

When I documented the remembrance work that absorbed the families of those who disappeared during the Pinochet dictatorship, and photographed archeologists engaged in forensic excavations, I was struck by the similarities between their approach and that of the photographer.
Likewise in Pompeii.

Disappearance, revelation, and development. Archeologists exhume memories from the earth, an episode in history.
Bodies that disappeared in Chile, Argentina, Bosnia, or Rwanda, or frescoes buried underground in Pompeii that regain the light of day—they all allow the descendants of the victims to get to know their history and thus form their identity. Thanks to the work of archeologists, historians and scientists can then reconstruct the origins and sequence of events more accurately, discover a material's components, and so on. Disappearance leads to many discoveries, revelations, and developments.

The charred pieces of wood will be analyzed to gather information on the 2019 fire as well as on the construction of the cathedral more than eight centuries ago.

Both archeologists and photographers are in search of memories and a form of truth.

Yet, the photographer makes the present moment disappear just to resurrect it in the form of an image that has already become part of the past. This is also a movement from disappearance to revelation and development. In the days when photos were still developed on photographic paper, an image would reappear in the photographer's stop bath.

From photographing men and women, I moved on to the traces buried underground. I became interested in the metaphorical landscapes of the Atacama Desert in Chile, where the sinister Caravan of Death passed under Pinochet's watch.

When, on April 15, 2019, I watched the inferno that ravaged Notre-Dame de Paris, I became an immediate witness to the possible disappearance of a part of our heritage and our collective memory, of a symbol of Paris and its identity.

The cathedral as seen from the
Pont de l'Archevêché in December 2019

This emotion I felt and shared with all Parisians and all those present during this dramatic event, as well as with the TV audiences in France and around the world, gradually transformed into a desire to document the reconstruction of the cathedral.

A Changing
Point of View

On the 22 Brumaire of the year II of the French Republican calendar, the choral heart of the cathedral stopped beating. Songs no longer resonated under its vaults, incense no longer filled the vast space, its stained-glass windows no longer illuminated the eyes of those who frequented the church, and the Eucharist was no longer celebrated. The liturgical life of Notre-Dame had ceased to exist. On that 22 Brumaire, the cathedral was initially converted into a Temple of Reason. It is very difficult to see in this act anything other than a plain desecration, since it was put up for sale the following month, for it to be demolished. Yet, the revolutionaries' symbolic destructions were targeted and precise, and apart from a few sculptures and the imposing Gallery of Kings—which was taken down in those days—the structure of the cathedral itself did not suffer any substantial damage.

Two years later, in 1795, worship resumed, led by constitutional clergy, and the cathedral experienced what could only be called a renaissance. This raised a question that was both of a material and intellectual nature.

It was during those years that François-René du Chateaubriand began writing *The Genius of Christianity*, published in 1802—the year of the Concordat between France and the Vatican that solidified the Roman Catholic Church as the majority church of France and normalized relations again between the French state and the papacy. Although this essay is considered, alongside Victor Hugo's novel, to be one of the catalysts creating an awareness of the worth of medieval religious buildings for heritage purposes, the two authors' positions differ significantly.

Chateaubriand's text, written in exile during the French Revolution, boasts the virtues of Christianity as the foremost value of Gothic churches. Although he concedes that they have a certain amount of beauty, he argues that these buildings must be preserved because they are the reliquaries of the fervor of the centuries. He wrote this book, he writes, "to reinstall in these churches the pomp of worship and reemploy the servants of the altar," a goal eventually achieved through the Concordat, as he concludes: "*The Genius of Christianity* now seems to be independent of the circumstances to which it may owe some of its success. . . . The altars were resurrected, the priests returned from their banishment, the prelates resumed their roles as principal dignitaries of the state." The purpose of this book was to defend the value of a place, not that of the Gothic cathedral as a building.

Since the beginning of the seventeenth century, a distinction has been made between two types of medieval churches: those that represented the old Gothic style and those that stood for a new Gothic era. The former were then, from 1820 onward, labeled as Romanesque churches, and the latter as Gothic houses of worship. The difference between these two styles revolves around the notion of a *secular school* that would come to characterize a new approach in architecture and became an idea widely used in nineteenth-century writing, especially by Viollet-le-Duc.

Thus, the architects of Gothic buildings were no longer considered to be holy men from a monastic world but engineers in a civil society. Thanks to their freedom and great independence of thought, so the assumption, they revolutionized the knowledge of construction techniques by erecting buildings of an unprecedented scale.

According to these new semantics, these two categories of church types and their architects were no longer only distinct, but virtually opposed to one another. However, this idealized vision came up against two contradictions.

First, as Prosper Mérimée noted, the Romanesque and the Gothic were not clearly distinguished styles that separated at a junction, so they cannot be considered opposing traditions: "The two styles, so different in appearance when we consider them each at one point of their development, merge almost imperceptibly at their transition point."

Second, many enormous buildings, built much earlier, had already supplanted what this supposed secular school is said to have produced in its first decades, notably the abbey of Cluny III and Speyer Cathedral in Germany, with vaults the same height as Notre-Dame de Paris, despite having been erected a century earlier.

This secularization did not affect just the issue of architects. The concomitance of the construction of these large cathedrals and the rise of cities has led some authors to name the latter among the driving forces behind or even the instigators of these building projects. Mérimée wrote, "Now, we will see princes, cities, even nations come together to erect cathedrals." As a result, the raison d'être of cathedrals was considered to have both civil and religious motifs. Their liturgical function is sometimes even completely pushed aside, as in Viollet-le-Duc's novel *Histoire d'un hôtel de ville et d'une cathédrale* (*History of a Town Hall and a Cathedral*). In it, the building appears separated from the institution of the church; the confiscation of the church's property is, so to speak, complete.

This emancipation can be observed from the 1830s onward in the writings of Victor Hugo, for whom "there are two things in an edifice: its use and its beauty. Its use belongs to the owner, its beauty to everyone" (translated by Danny Smith). We read between the lines that the architectural work need not concern the matters of the church. It is this kind of beauty that Notre-Dame embodies, and that the austere and sly Monseigneur Claude Frollo, the prelate of the Catholic Church in *The Hunchback of Notre Dame*, rejects.

Thus, if for Chateaubriand the church was a place, for Hugo it is an object without any real connection to its use. It is, in this case, the object that interests the poet, which marks a major turning point in how intellectuals regard cathedrals. It is during that period that the objet d'art gradually comes into being. This development set in with the French Revolution, when objects that had been seized from churches were redistributed across the country, without any consideration of their regional roots or, a fortiori, their use. Only a few of these objects were returned to Notre-Dame for religious purposes in 1795, and when the matter was reopened in 1843 at the request of the French minister of religious affairs, the Commission on Historical Monuments (Commission des monuments historiques) authorized the return of the funeral objects and buildings in question only in exceptional circumstances, fearing that this would set a precedent. The commission stated that "pieces of art are better placed for research in museums, where they can be collected and receive greater exposure than in churches, where they are scattered and often shut away in safes."

On another level, Notre-Dame de Paris is further marked by major urban transformations. The cathedral square was opened up and its surrounding area was developed, including the Rue du Cloître-Notre-Dame and the gardens behind the apsis and the demolition of the former Hôtel-Dieu main hospital. The cathedral was no longer a place filled with life in the heart of the city, but became an object of contemplation and admiration; that is to say, an objet d'art.

This evolution of the gaze is further fueled by well-known artists, writers, architects, and sculptors. Auguste Rodin is one of them, whose *Cathedrals of France* (1914; translated by Elisabeth Chase Geissbuhler) makes no reference whatsoever to the liturgical role played by these buildings. It is therefore not surprising that the term "cathedral" has come to equally designate

churches that are or have been episcopal sees, and those that have never served that purpose. This is particularly the case for the collegiate churches of Mantes-la-Jolie, Melun, and even Saint-Étienne of Nevers, which is not in fact the cathedral of the eponymous city. This is not just a question of literary rhetoric: even the Commission on Historical Monuments uses the term "cathedral" in its minutes from June 21, 1845, to refer to the royal chapel Sainte-Chapelle in the Palais de la Cité.

These were more than subconscious adaptations, as Joris-Karl Huysmans's stirring words from the early twentieth century show: "All these architects, all these archaeologists, from Viollet-le-Duc to Quicherat, saw in the ogival basilica nothing more but a stone body; they were simultaneously physiologists and historians, but this eventually led to what could be called the materialism of historic buildings. They considered only the shell and the bark; they obsessed over the body and forgot the soul."

Who even remembers that the term "cathedral" designates an episcopal see? Detached from its etymology, the term has become profane. In the eyes of the nineteenth century, enriched by the gaze of heritage, the cathedral found itself simultaneously stripped of a part of itself, the one that was its original raison d'être. However, these two perspectives are not mutually exclusive, and the resonances they create can only add to the attraction of this place.

A Human Adventure
Summer 2019–Summer 2020

Tuesday, July 2, 2019. Everyone is on-site today to witness the first of the twenty-eight centerings being raised that will support the flying buttresses: the craftspeople, General Georgelin, the engineers, and the architects, including Philippe Villeneuve, as well as rector Monseigneur Chauvet. Everyone is holding their breath. The tension is palpable.

Philippe Villeneuve was appointed chief architect for historical monuments (ACMH) in 2013 and is in charge of the cathedral of Notre-Dame de Paris; in this capacity, he oversees the restoration works.

Monseigneur Patrick Chauvet is the appointed
rector of the cathedral.

Each of the fifty-two centerings overall weighs about 8 tons, and in addition to being magnificent objects in themselves, they are high-precision engineering works, designed to the nearest millimeter.

Rope access technicians during the installment of the twenty-eight centerings to support the flying buttresses

The center of gravity of each of the centerings has been calculated so that they are balanced when being raised, and so that each one can be maneuvered between two flying buttresses before being fitted underneath the one they are designed to support. All this is orchestrated by a young man called Mehdi: using his walkie-talkie, he guides the crane operator and carpenters who are executing the operation high above our heads. It is really impressive to watch.

Wednesday, January 15, 2020. Since the site was reopened at the end of August, there has been a considerable increase in the number of safety instructions relating to the presence of lead and the risk of collapse. The site is split into two zones: one is clean, and the other polluted. We enter through the first, where we store all our city clothes, including our underwear, in lockers.

Visitors like me are provided with white hazmat suits and disposable underwear, in addition to a helmet, gloves, and mandatory safety shoes. Every time I leave the site, I have to take a shower wearing all this: the suit, helmet, gloves, shoes, and respirator mask, if I used one. Everything has to pass through the shower, my camera included (which I wrap in a plastic cover). Afterward, I have to throw

away the suit, the gloves, and the underwear straight from the shower through an opening into a plastic bag. Through the second airlock, I return to the clean zone, but naked as a jaybird. I put my city clothes back on. I particularly admire the rope access technicians because they wear a complex full mask almost all the time, as well as a climbing and a safety harness, and tools—and they weigh a ton!

What's impressive: when they are roped up, they look like astronauts in space. They become light, dance in the air, float. They are always absolutely focused. Absentmindedness would be fatal.

Wednesday, August 12, 2020. I went to the site in the evening to photograph the operations that take place at night, such as using a very high-efficiency vacuum cleaner on a land-loaded truck from which dozens of feet of hose are unrolled that reach up to the transept to suck up the dust and small bits of debris underneath the vaults. Unfortunately, due to thunderstorms, this operation was canceled that night. Instead, I was able to photograph the rope access technicians by day as they were securing stones from the vaults of the northern transept and recovering further bits of wood, metal, and coal. It was a pretty sporty and physically tiring endeavor.

Rope access technicians at the northern transept are securing some stones damaged by the fire.

I reconnect with the stonemasons I had met and photographed right at the start of the project. One calls out to me through his full-face respirator: "Patrick, aren't you gonna say hi anymore?" I look at him but don't recognize him. "We're the stonemasons. You photographed us at the beginning of the works!" Unbelievable! They went on a rope access training course to be able to return to the site where their stone-masonry job had come to an end. I remember them well. They were a fine team of jolly fellows from the Pyrenees. We are happy to meet again and recall not-so-distant memories that seem to us, in view of the progress of this project, as if they already belonged to the past and a different era.

I take some shots in the locker room, have a shower, get rid of all my disposable clothes, and rinse my Canon wrapped in plastic, as well as my helmet, and my safety shoes from which I have removed the paper overshoes.

I meet Grégory, one of the leaders of the rope access technician team, who asks me, "So you're still around, Patrick? What did you snap?" I tell him, and he looks pleased. The rope access technicians take pride in their profession, and they have every reason to: without them, none of this would be possible. They are the heroes of this extraordinary worksite.

Initially, Grégory was rather suspicious of me and called me very formally Mr. Zachmann. It must be said that at that point, I did not yet know all the safety instructions and had not yet received training on lead safety, so I made mistakes. But over time and after having seen several publications featuring my photos, I think he now respects me. He is no longer formal with me and is happy to inform me about upcoming plans. He is always on-site—and always in a good mood!

A VIEW FROM HISTORY BY OLIVIER DE CHÂLUS

Historical Monuments, A Saga

In 1841, a collective consisting of Monseigneur Affre, the archbishop of Paris, Victor Hugo, Jean-Auguste-Dominique Ingres, Alfred de Vigny, and Charles Forbes René de Montalembert were up in arms about the deplorable state the Parisian cathedral was in. Their movement gathered momentum that eventually led to plans for a substantial renovation project, and a design competition the following year, won by the architects Eugène Viollet-le-Duc and Jean-Baptiste Lassus.

The competition was judged by the Council for Civil Buildings, of which Viollet-le-Duc was a member and whose director was a close acquaintance of his father's. Prosper Mérimée, a good friend of both Viollet-le-Duc and Lassus, was also among the judges. The project was signed off by the Chamber of Peers, the parliamentary upper house at that time, whose members included Victor Hugo and Montalembert. So the saga of this restoration project begins, which would conclude twenty years later with the consecration of the cathedral and its classification as a historical monument.

Was the cathedral really in such bad condition? Regular maintenance work had in fact been undertaken throughout the eighteenth century. The choir had been remodeled, the vault of the transept crossing had been refurbished, the frame had been cleaned up and whitewashed, and the paving had been redone. With the exception of the rose windows, all the stained-glass windows had been replaced, a new organ installed, and the central portal modified. The greatest architects and artists had been entrusted with this work. Extensive work had even been carried out around the cathedral, affecting the bishop's palace, the sacristy, the main hospital Hôtel-Dieu, and other buildings.

The cathedral seemed in a state of repair that would help it survive for centuries to come—some people at the time even complained it looked too new. The French Revolution caused damage to the cathedral, though in reality the attacks were very targeted and affected mainly the statuary. Noteworthy is also that the medieval spire was dismantled at that time to avoid collapse, and to protect the building as a whole.

Far from being neglected, Notre-Dame de Paris became, in the early nineteenth century, the French nation's church. It was here that the signing of the Concordat was celebrated in 1802, as was the coronation of Napoleon in 1804. Flags that the French Grande Armée had taken from enemy armies were hung in the nave, and one celebratory *Te Deum* after another was sung, from the Napoleonic Wars to the victories of Louis XVIII in the Battle of Trocadero in 1823, and of Charles X at Algiers in 1830.

Royal births, baptisms, weddings, and funerals were celebrated in the cathedral, requiring changes to the décor, ornamentation, and liturgy. Each of these ceremonies demonstrated such a high degree of dramatization that it leads one to believe these must have been temporary events, hastily put together, comparable to an opera set. Yet, the preparations would take months and were carried out under the systematic guidance of renowned architects.

One example: the carpet for the baptism of Charles X's grandson in 1842, measuring 2,066 square feet (192 square meters), was eight years in the making.

This litany of events and maintenance works undertaken makes the need for a sudden redevelopment unlikely, and nothing suggests that the building was in danger. However, when our modern-day eyes gaze upon the few photographs and daguerreotypes that exist prior to the great restoration, the repairs appear very necessary indeed.

With the Concordat of 1801, which came into force in 1802, the Catholic clergy was integrated into the French public administrative body: they managed the diocese's heritage sites. The bishops, the "best judges of that which befits religious ceremonies in cathedrals," thus became the patrons of the maintenance and other works to be undertaken, and received, where appropriate, financial support from the central administration via the prefects. Together, they could henceforth appoint an architect of their choice. The management of cathedrals was therefore largely decentralized.

From 1810, Notre-Dame de Paris was thus entrusted to architect Alexandre-Théodore Brongniart, replaced in 1813 by Étienne-Hippolyte Godde.

In the first quarter of the nineteenth century, the works carried out did not follow a concerted plan and had a definite liturgical bend. For the first time, in 1824, a national program was launched to counteract the risk of damage. Lightning rods were installed and buildings were removed that were crammed into densely built-up urban centers. The first spark for a national policy for the maintenance of religious assets had thus been ignited, but at this stage it did not yet trigger an appetite for the protection of heritage sites. In the early 1830s, as Victor Hugo's novel was being printed, the Commission on Historical Monuments was finally established, and it would be instituted in 1837. It denounced the lack of architects skilled in traditional medieval building techniques, and advocated for the employment of specialists, recruited from a Parisian hub that it administered. For example, Godde was accused of employing techniques that did not comply with the overall structure, and for his lack of respect for the artistic merit of the cathedral, since he was influenced mainly by Romantic ideals.

In 1848, an organization of specialized architects was created, whose successors are the current body of heritage architects, and the chief architects for historical monuments (ACMH). In parallel, the policies for intervention still in existence were gradually established. The aim of the Commission on Historical Monuments was to exercise architectural control over the buildings it added to its list. It defined the scope of the projects under its auspices and subsidized them, sometimes in full. Financing, decision-making, and the choice of the prime contractors became centralized—and thus, a national heritage policy emerged within which the old generation, that of Godde, no longer had a place.

In this context, the knowledge and understanding of historical buildings became essential. But with very few writings surviving from medieval times, nineteenth-century architects owed their knowledge to the analysis of the building itself. The greatest researchers, therefore, traveled up and down the country—Viollet-le-Duc and Mérimée in particular. Important buildings were methodically identified, surveyed, and described according to specifically designed methods. The emerging technology of photography was one of the leading new technologies employed for this undertaking. Archeology congresses were organized and the conference proceedings published to facilitate a regular exchange between scholars. From 1834 onward, the *Bulletin monumental* would allow scholars to regularly share research advances within their field.

Faced with new considerations, the emerging scientific community needed to expand its terminology to describe its object of study. Its vocabulary is certainly ornate yet also unexpectedly generalized. The word "transept," for example, did not appear in the French language until 1820, to refer to the part of a church that gives its floor plan the shape of a cross. The word makes it possible to describe the formal aspects of the building feature, but not to distinguish transepts that end in semicircles from those with large portals at the ends, and whose liturgical roles necessarily differ from one another. This is just one example of the vocabulary we inherited that is very suited to describe an architectural feature but less so to learn about its technical and functional aspects.

The only facts we have about the cathedral's state of disrepair in 1842 come from supporters of the restoration project or are derived from a few images. There is nothing to confirm that the building was in jeopardy. On the other hand, as far as one can judge from the images, in terms of it being a "historical monument," a restoration was desperately necessary. This work would be undertaken by a young generation: Viollet-le-Duc was twenty-nine years old, and Lassus thirty-six years of age; Mérimée was forty years old, and Victor Hugo, forty-one—a generation that would impose its vision of heritage on the redesign of institutions and impose a new doctrinal approach on religious buildings.

The Great Scaffolding Challenge
December 2019–November 2020

Wednesday, December 4, 2019. I decide to check out the northern side. We go up and down the numerous steps of two spiral staircases. I ask my "security man" where he is from. Tlemcem, Algeria, he replies. I tell him that I know the city because my mother grew up in Aïn Témouchent, not far from his hometown, and that my great-grandfather was a rabbi there. Actually, I didn't tell him that bit; I only thought about it. And I recalled the emotion I felt when I went to the Jewish cemetery in Tlemcen, with a guard close by my side who helped me look for the grave of my great-grandfather Abraham Bensamoun. All of a sudden, he had exclaimed victoriously: "Abraham Bensamoun! I found it!" He had wiped over it, and inscriptions in Hebrew and French had emerged.

We arrive at the top, and here I meet the "north" team of scaffolders. Jolly fellows. One of them, a Sicilian, is chatting on about the lunch they are going to have and that their wives were apparently preparing for them. I write down the email address of one of them to send them some photos.

I play around with the graphic lines of the scaffolding and press the trigger when one or more craftspeople appear, seen through the tubes.

Some 200 tons of scaffolding tubes that had been erected before the fire of April 15, 2019, have to be dismantled.

Thursday, January 9, 2020, 12:45 p.m. I went back into the cathedral, but nothing was happening there. There was no one there.

The plan yesterday was to photograph the rope access technicians clearing the southern loft. But Grégory, one of the team leaders, told me at the last minute that this had been canceled due to scaffolding works. I did not fully understand why, but something to do with security reasons.

So I spontaneously asked the manager of the scaffolding team, Franck, if I could hop on the aerial work platform and go up with them. I had to climb onto the platform located next to the east wall of the cathedral's north side, but just as we were about to be lifted, I was told that the weight of the load of steel tubes and bolts on their own would be too heavy, so I couldn't go up with them.

So I climbed into the other aerial work platform, on the west side. I waited almost an hour with the driver of the AWP and two very nice, friendly guys for the crane next to us to finish loading and unloading. A traffic jam of cranes.

Once up there, I was able to take pretty impressive shots of them clambering across the outer western side of the scaffolding that was half scorched by the fire, with a heap of charred debris underneath. The gray light was fading, but I really like this monochrome, almost black-and-white palette.

Craftspeople are securing the damaged scaffolding to prevent it
from slipping during the extensive dismantling works.

Thursday, January 9, 2020, 12:45 p.m. I went back into the cathedral, but nothing was happening there. There was no one there.

The plan yesterday was to photograph the rope access technicians clearing the southern loft. But Grégory, one of the team leaders, told me at the last minute that this had been canceled due to scaffolding works. I did not fully understand why, but something to do with security reasons.

So I spontaneously asked the manager of the scaffolding team, Franck, if I could hop on the aerial work platform and go up with them. I had to climb onto the platform located next to the east wall of the cathedral's north side, but just as we were about to be lifted, I was told that the weight of the load of steel tubes and bolts on their own would be too heavy, so I couldn't go up with them.

So I climbed into the other aerial work platform, on the west side. I waited almost an hour with the driver of the AWP and two very nice, friendly guys for the crane next to us to finish loading and unloading. A traffic jam of cranes.

Once up there, I was able to take pretty impressive shots of them clambering across the outer western side of the scaffolding that was half scorched by the fire, with a heap of charred debris underneath. The gray light was fading, but I really like this monochrome, almost black-and-white palette.

Thursday, March 5, 2020. I can finally photograph General Georgelin on-site, as per my request. I am not alone; there is also a television news team, whose director I met the previous day—a very nice man. At 2:30 p.m., I am already kitted out in my astronaut suit with my fanny pack around the waist, containing my camera and various essentials such as spare batteries, memory cards, a notebook, a pen, and my cell phone, I have a harness underneath, and a rucksack on my back. Together with the television team, I am waiting for the general to arrive. I have been keeping an eye on the weather forecast, which predicts rain starting at 3:30 p.m. When we can finally get into the AWP basket after several photo shoots in other places, it is about 4:00 p.m.: the sky is full of threatening gray rain clouds. I take a photo of the general in front of one end of the northern façade. Then we rise to the highest point that the weather conditions and the crane transportation allow. I take photos with this feeling well known to photographers; namely, that we are capturing important photos for history and the media. My lens is sprinkled with droplets that I wipe off at regular intervals.

Monday, June 8, 2020. On the radio this morning, I hear today's headlines: "Aerial Acrobatics at Notre Dame," "A Delicate Game of Pick Up Sticks." This morning, at 9:00, the dismantling operation will commence, prizing apart 200 tons of scaffolding that had virtually melted the night of the fire and that now blocks access to some parts of the cathedral. Already delayed because of lead contamination, bad weather, and the COVID-19 lockdown, this complex and unprecedented operation, a real "puzzle," is said to take until the fall.

The scaffolding had been erected before the fire as part of the restoration works on the spire. Its dismantling is crucial to saving the cathedral. It is only after this stage that architects and experts will be able to work out the condition of the vaulted ceiling, assess its stability, and confirm if Notre-Dame is safe from collapse. This moment, which many have long been waiting for, is risky because many fear that removing parts of this huge "pick-up-sticks game" will cause the entire scaffolding to collapse, and with it the arches of the vaulted ceiling. That is why the old half-charred scaffolding was stabilized and strengthened by centering it.

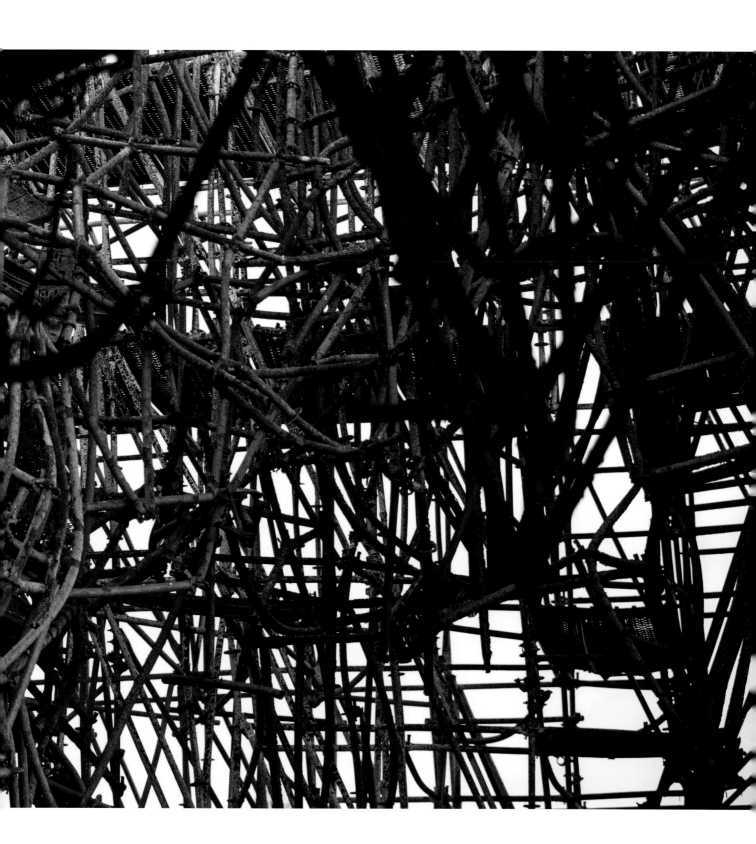

Early in the morning, I went out on the frame floor of the scaffolding to make
the most of the beautiful low-angled light. I was able to take beautiful shots of
the rope access technicians descending into this colossus of burned and entangled
steel. They left shortly afterward to go on their break before tackling the task

of cutting up the old scaffolding. That's when I was asked to step back, as a safety precaution. When I arrived back home that night, I was physically completely exhausted: my legs and thighs were aching because I had been squatting for hours while trying not to move my 400 mm zoom lens too much.

Rope access technicians are carrying out
tests before dismantling the scaffolding.

Wednesday, June 10, 2020. The elevator operator spends all his time either going up and down or waiting. So, since I am spending quite some time with him, we develop a relationship! At one point, he starts singing "Si j'étais riche . . ." ("If I were rich . . .") by Les Rita Mitsouko. He then tells me, "If only I won five million in the lottery!" I reply, "One million wouldn't be too bad for a start." He: "No, that's not enough. I want to buy myself a house and a beautiful car and go traveling."

Christophe, my crane buddy, accompanied me in the elevator for the first 164 feet (50 meters). I had to climb the last 98 feet (30 meters) by myself, which was not very reassuring. From up there the view is fantastic, and thanks to the 100-400 mm zoom my Canon affords me, I have a bird's-eye view, and at the same time I get a close-up view that allows me to photograph details of the rope access technicians at work. I watch them as they cut through the singed steel tubes. It is impressive to see them among this assemblage of tubes—200 tons in all.

Construction Works, Their Duration, and Anachronisms

It would take until late 2020 for the cathedral to be freed from the scaffolding that had been erected to restore the spire. This meticulous dismantling project certainly reminds us of medieval construction works and their very long durations. According to a legend from the late Middle Ages, the construction of Notre-Dame de Paris began in 1163 and took 107 or 160 years to be completed, depending on whether you take the completion of the works on the transept or that of the apse chapels as your reference.

In popular culture, the expression "It would take 107 years" eventually prevailed in reference to the impressive amount of time it took to construct this church. The length may sound surprising when you consider, for example, that the construction of the choir of the abbey church of Saint-Denis in the mid-twelfth century took only four years, that the large buildings of Royaumont and Chaalis Abbey from the early thirteenth century were completed in seven and nineteen years, respectively, and that at the end of the eleventh century, the abbey of Cluny III, the largest church in the medieval world, was erected in just twenty-five years.

There are several hypotheses to justify the speed of these works, notably the influence of the monasteries, the affluence of the dioceses, and support from the Crown. But what has not been noted up until now is that these churches have an important fact in common: none of them have survived to the present day. Conversely, the better a church is preserved, the longer the duration of the construction work we associate with it—generally in the region of a minimum of eighty years for large buildings.

The consecration of the altar of Notre-Dame de Paris—that is to say, the moment when its liturgical use began—took place in 1182. Research in the late nineteenth and early twentieth centuries deduced that the choir and therefore the vaults must have been completed on that date. This implies that the cathedral must have featured flying buttresses in the twelfth century, which did not survive. It was also partly to justify their replacement that Viollet-le-Duc invented the devastating fire he described in his *Dictionnaire*.

It was only after its restoration in the nineteenth century that Notre-Dame de Paris was consecrated, in 1864, and formally made a place of worship. Similarly, the recent cathedrals of Évry and Créteil were consecrated only after their construction had been completed, in 1995 and 2015, respectively. Modern-day logic, therefore, puts these stages of the building projects in sequential order, separating the time of the construction from that of worship, since this seems natural to us.

When the building does not provide them with any further clues, researchers have no other source of information but ancient writings, which very rarely evoke construction sites but instead focus on recounting ceremonies. It is through reference to these, and the assumption that they imply that the works had been completed earlier, that the singularly short time frames I mentioned above were calculated.

However, abundant evidence that liturgy and construction works coexisted in the Middle Ages contradicts these calculations. This is particularly the case for Saint-Denis in the twelfth century, where a storm was reported during mass, when the abbey church did not yet have a vault. A century later, the scaffolding for the new choir of this church collapsed onto the monks who were celebrating mass. William of Donjeon, archbishop of Bourges, died in 1209 celebrating mass in a choir open to the elements. And how could the thief responsible for the 1218 fire in Notre-Dame have tried to steal the candlesticks of the altar from the loft if the choir had had a vault?

In fact, medieval construction projects were carried out over long periods of time. We know that in the case of Notre-Dame de Paris, construction began between 1160, the date of the election of Maurice de Sully as bishop, and 1163, the date on which the construction site is first mentioned in the chronicles. If we consider the building of the choir chapels as the point of completion of the works, the construction would have lasted nearly 160 years. This length of time certainly seems abstract if we consider it as taking place over centuries that make up the historical past. But ten medieval years are no shorter than ten years in the early twenty-first century. Therefore, we would only have to imagine a construction site that would have started in the days of Napoleon and would have been completed today—

which is almost exactly the same amount of years it is taking to build Sagrada Familia in Barcelona, or a construction site started in 1960 that would be completed around 2120.

How to explain such a long time frame, in a dynamic medieval world with constant new technological and intellectual innovations? Land negotiations, clearing land previously occupied by other buildings while maintaining a continuity of liturgical service, laying foundations and carrying out earthworks, and obtaining timber for the roof truss are certainly among the necessary steps that best explain these very considerable time frames. The complexity of these issues is also relative to the proposed size of the church. The time it takes for the construction therefore naturally depends on the size of the planned building.

At the same time, the longer the project takes, the greater the likelihood of decision makers changing the plans. During that time, medieval society greatly advanced. The role of the bishops is turned upside down by the Gregorian Reforms, which would reverberate throughout the twelfth century; this was also reflected in the function of cathedrals, which necessarily had to evolve as well. The roles played by parishes were also redefined, in turn changing the purpose of cathedrals. Many theologians progressed Christian ideas, synods and councils multiplied, the way in which faith was practiced shifted, and one can reasonably assume that how it was celebrated changed alongside it. The cathedral planned when construction began is therefore probably not the one that was needed thirty years later, and even less so that which was required after completion.

It is in this context that we must undoubtedly consider the extension of the initial choir of Laon Cathedral, at the turn of the twelfth to the thirteenth century. It was in those years as well that the galleries of the cathedrals of Meaux and Rouen, whose exact function is unknown, were abandoned. A transept was eventually added to Notre-Dame at the beginning of the thirteenth century, probably to meet new liturgical demands.

Despite these redesigns and regular new construction works to realize these, we struggle nowadays to see in these large medieval churches anything other than homogeneous and coherent buildings cast in one piece. When depicting the works, in chronological order from the nineteenth century onward, with a colored map, we intuitively assume that these developments took place zone by zone, in complete blocks. However, there might be, for example, a significant time lag between the construction of the lower part of a façade and its upper section, even though a two-dimensional map may not distinguish between them. This is particularly the case for the Basilica of Saint-Denis, where, as soon as the construction was complete up to the height of the doors, work continued on the choir, with a view to a rapid consecration. Once again, usage took priority over the architectural coherence of the building.

There is therefore a constant back and forth in terms of the building works, with elements necessary for the functionality of the church taking precedence over nonessential work, which was sometimes postponed to later phases. The vaults of the cathedrals of Bourges and Amiens are noteworthy examples in this respect, since they were completed almost sixty years after the start of either of these building projects. At Notre-Dame de Paris, many clues also suggest that the vaults were installed at a very late stage.

Within large cathedrals, time lags abound, for a wide range of reasons. The oft-evoked harmony that is so important for the sacralization of a historical monument is therefore riddled with anachronisms. My aim here is of course not to reject this notion: the eye has its own sensibilities and habits, and the beauty it beholds in medieval churches is not up for debate. But it is a contemporaneous sense of beauty. The eyes of eighteenth-century people, such as Chateaubriand, found beauty elsewhere. From a medieval point of view, finally, we must consider the building from the point of view of the mason at the foot of the wall, looking up at a construction project that was subject to constant adjustments. What seems harmonious to us today must have sometimes appeared to these craftspeople to be tainted with unsightly adaptations.

Rediscovering Notre-Dame
May–November 2020

Friday, May 22, 2020. Construction has gradually resumed since lockdown, from April 27 onward, and I'm able to return to the site today. It is nice, especially since I am the only media person allowed to enter.

After having spent a good amount of time at "base camp" (that is, in the "clean" zone), I went to get ready in the locker rooms. Nothing has changed, really. Once I have undressed and equipped myself with a new kind of hazmat suit that also covers the shoes—which is much more convenient than the one before—as well as a helmet, my camera, and a harness, and have put a respirator mask in my backpack, I pass through the airlock and enter the "polluted" zone. It is weird because I feel safer here than in the "clean" zone, where COVID-19 is raging. As if it was nonexistent here. We are so well protected from lead that I feel invulnerable!

Moreover, the training I received on the risks of high blood lead levels and on the safety protocol on-site (showering, decontaminating everything that was in the "dirty" zone, washing hands for a long time, etc.) helped me manage our new life living with the virus.

New scaffolding was installed around the damaged older structure, to allow for it to be dissembled.

I recognize the Alsatian, then the guy called "the Sicilian" by his colleagues, and a few others from afar, hanging from the scaffolding tubes of the elevator under construction.

I take a few pictures and report to the security booth because I have to be accompanied by a guard. Désiré, who is originally from the Ivory Coast, is waiting for me and welcomes me with a broad smile. He did not leave his post once during lockdown. He poses for me with the keys to access all areas of the cathedral, including that to the large gate that opens up onto cathedral square, and tells me, proudly and with a smirk, "I'm the keeper of the temple."

I decide to start shooting high up from the elevator of the scaffolding. We go up to the south transept, from where I have a very graphic overview, complete with several balancing scaffolders. I stay for quite a while. Désiré gets impatient. So, I explain to him why we have to wait a long time to take a good shot; in this case, it is a question of composition and placement of the various people and graphic elements within the frame. He understands and starts tapping on his smartphone keyboard.

The scaffolding is being assembled for the installation of an elevator to access the upper levels of the site.

We leave this viewpoint to join the rope access technicians who have to clean the belfry of the southern tower. I hope to see the bells because I have never photographed them before. The technicians have just arrived and are waiting for the key to be let in through the door. They all are sitting in a row, wearing surgical masks. I take a picture of the bells of the north tower, including Gabriel, the largest one, and follow the rope access technicians toward the entrance to the southern belfry. Mathieu, their team leader, tells me that I can't go in without a full-face mask. I take pictures of them making preparations, and leave when they start cleaning the walls. Too much lead dust. And with a full-face mask on, I can't see through the viewfinder. The only solution is to use the digital screen, but since I am farsighted, I have to wear glasses to see close-up . . . it's too complicated. So, instead, I usually wear a "pig nose" mask that does not cover my eyes.

I take a picture of them in front of a large bell, climbing up toward the wooden ceiling. A photo that makes you think of "Spider-Man"! I have to work fast. Fortunately, I brought my wide-angle zoom with me, the 20-35 mm on top of the 24-70 mm, because the 20 mm is my only option to fit the entire huge bell and all the rope access technicians into the shot. I can't take too much equipment with me, and I had to choose between this wide-angle and a telephoto lens. I made the right choice. It is dark despite the cinema "festoons" they installed at the back to light up the space. I have to work with a 4,000 ASA film with little depth of focus. I stop and leave as soon as they start cleaning, as agreed on.

I am finally able to go up on an aerial work platform. A rope access technician team leader has agreed to accompany me. I don't recognize him right away, but he tells me at the outset that "I was the one you photographed on the north tower." He is talking about the famous photo of two rope access technicians climbing up the façade of the north tower. I ask him if he saw the photo, which was recently exhibited along the fence. "Yes, of course." He thanks me.

The other day, I passed by the left bank in front of Notre-Dame. Boxed in by all the scaffolding, the cathedral looks like a big wounded creature covered up with bandages.

Wednesday, November 18, 2020. I go to the site to take pictures at night. It's magical! I photograph from the aerial work platform, from the frame floors along the choir and the nave, and from the north tower. I witness the final stage of dismantling the scorched scaffolding and see the new one being erected, which will form a securing brace around the old one. It's impressive: the work is completed without the slightest mishap. The atmosphere is joyous. The whole team has managed to meet the main challenge of securing Our Lady. I end the evening accompanied by a security guard with whom I climb to the top of the north tower. The tower crane is lit up, as is a section of the construction site, and with Paris behind it, it's a stunning sight.

Didier Cuiset, the director of the scaffolding company Europe Échafaudage, is proud of his team, and always full of energy. He joins in at the coalface and glides between the scaffolding bars effortlessly and with incredible agility. He

offers to take a picture of me sitting on a guardrail that runs along the huge hole at the transept. I secure myself with my harness—looks like I'll get a picture of myself after all!

Frédérique Meyer, the press relations manager, called me back to tell me that I could finally photograph the removal of the last console that held up the scaffolding. When the console was lifted by the tower crane, we had to leave the frame floor as a safety precaution, since the console was going to pass over our heads. So we all waited on the ground, at the foot of the cathedral, level with the choir, for the console to be passed over us. Or rather, I photographed the group looking up into the air. The next day, I returned to take pictures from the top of the tower crane, capturing the entire cathedral and the transept crossing, now rid of its scaffolding. The view of Paris was breathtaking.

In Search of Authenticity

Nineteenth-century restorers largely claimed to have remained faithful to the buildings in their care. Lassus and Viollet-le-Duc make a particular point of this when speaking about their plans for Notre-Dame de Paris: "We believe that each section added in any given era must in principle be preserved, secured, and restored in the style that befits it, while exercising religious discretion and denying oneself any personal opinion." But this principle was hardly followed to the letter.

First of all, the transept roof truss has been replaced, without taking notes or describing the previous work. Lassus and Viollet-le-Duc also tried to erase the modifications that had been made to the building throughout history. Thus, some of the windows that had been redone in the thirteenth century were dismantled, to be replaced with windows they imagined the cathedral would have had in the twelfth century. They also modified the axis of the south rose window and rebuilt its entire structure, to correct an eighteenth-century restoration they judged clumsily done.

Many aspects of these restorations are questionable, but on the whole they tried to bring us closer to an authentically medieval cathedral. Conversely, some authentic elements were also removed during the restoration. Particularly the windows of the gallery, which they recognized as being medieval but which did not belong to "any style" and were thus replaced with windows conforming to the medieval forms promoted in the nineteenth century. The plans for the spire, which, during the restoration works, developed further and further away from the archival material available about medieval steeples, followed the same logic of idealization. The restorer consciously wished to embellish the cathedral with an object that did not belong to its history, but instead sought to bring it in line with the image of the Middle Ages to which people of the time aspired. One might call this a "neo-Gothization" of Notre-Dame de Paris.

In addition to these modifications that ostensibly affected the cathedral's shape, there have been other, more-discreet ones. One notable example is that the vaults of the galleries located near the façade were raised. The fire that Viollet-le-Duc imagined to justify a series of modifications to Notre-Dame in the thirteenth century could not have caused the damage he cites without an earlier, quite substantial alteration to the cathedral, which particularly concerned the type of vaults above the galleries. The fact that there were no genuine vestiges of the supposed fire, and that no examples of the imagined configuration existed anywhere else, weakened his theory. It was probably for this reason that the evidence itself, which did not appear on any documentation prior to the restoration, was incorporated into the building. The process was effective: this lack of authenticity was not identified until the 1990s. It was no longer the case of Viollet-le-Duc, a historian, leading the restoration works, but of the restorer rewriting history.

This approach finds its counterpart in the literature, where, regardless of the lack of evidence, Viollet-le-Duc sometimes claimed to understand medieval building methods better than the workers of the Middle Ages who employed them. In the article "Tas-de-charge" in his *Dictionnaire*, about the lower courses of ribs of a Gothic vault, we find the following: "It is in accordance with this theory [of the tas-de-charge] that the exceedingly interesting church Notre-Dame de Dijon was built. Unfortunately, its parsimonious execution, undertaken by workers who did not fully conceive of the adopted system, leaves much to be desired. The design is nevertheless very remarkable and owed to a skilled master."

Two characters merge in this figure of the learned master: the first is that of the restorer as a member of the organization of specialized architects formed in 1848 to care for these historical monuments; this former bases his legitimacy on his claim to being the heir to a second figure he himself created, that of the architect belonging to the secular school. Parallels abound between these figures and can be spotted in the anachronisms that nowadays appear rather glaring. How come Viollet-le-Duc's novel *Histoire d'un hôtel de ville et d'une cathédrale* does not mention the competition that took place to restore Notre-Dame de Paris? To rebuild his cathedral, the fictional bishop of Clusy, whose finances are limited, turns to the civil authorities. The master architects who were called to compete present projects in the vein of the complete freedom attributed to architects of the secular school. The election of Jean d'Orbais seems a given (like that of real-life Jean Jacques Nicolas Arveuf-Fransquin for Notre-Dame de Paris), but the dark horse Hugues de Courtenay presents, according to the illustrations of the novel, a project similar in every way to Viollet-le-Duc's ideal cathedral and triumphantly wins the tender.

The way in which nineteenth-century architects regarded medieval architects was hence clearly lacking in objectivity: they would indeed consider that each medieval "architect" had freed himself from established technical rules and was working in complete independence. However, if we do not always manage to account for each of the techniques used, that is because we are familiar with only some of the construction principles governing the Middle Ages. Only by readjusting the truthfulness of our gaze on medieval building structures can we rediscover these builders.

We don't know much about medieval master builders. The only contract of the time in question that has been passed down to us is that given to the master Gautier de Varinfroy, who was entrusted with "executing the construction work" of the cathedral of Meaux in 1253. This document states that "he will not have the right to go to the site of Évreux or any other construction site." But what does "executing the construction work" mean? Does "work" refer to the building as a whole, or only his substantial but concise task? Does the task with which he was entrusted include the design of the work or simply its realization? Does it cover its financial management? Logistical issues? We don't know any more than that.

The term "architect" was not used in the Middle Ages, and, as is usually the case, Gautier de Varinfroy is referred to as "master," a term that is generally associated with that of a master builder in its contemporaneous sense and by extension to an architect as described in the nineteenth century. We can also compare him to similar people, notably Renaud de Cormont, who was called to the cathedral of Amiens at the age of seventeen. But how could he alone have borne the responsibility for these maintenance works, given his young age, when he could not have had the necessary experience? Similarly, how could Gautier de Varinfroy have foreseen the new building techniques to come, such as the installation of vaults, if he was not allowed to go and learn elsewhere how to construct these?

In the Middle Ages, the term "master" simply referred to a recognized expert in their field. Some were master masons, iron craftspeople, locksmiths, or carpenters; others were master builders; others still were so-called magister operis, etc. These designations tell us something about the great diversity of skills in the world of medieval-building craftsmanship. Clergymen turned to these masters for their expert opinions when they believed that technical questions needed to be discussed, which is proof of their ability to comprehend and make decisions. Some master builders were also accompanied by specialists; their technical skills were therefore complementary, which contradicts the idea of an omniscient architect and highlights that many more people worked on medieval construction sites, which were hence much more collective endeavors than the nineteenth century wanted to believe.

Goldsmiths and Beekeepers
January–December 2020

Friday, January 10, 2020. I was able to slip into the marquees where the stones, wood, and metal parts are stored and sorted that have been recovered from the fire. I caught up with archeologists and researchers from the Research Laboratory for Historical Monuments (LRMH), who know me well. The marquees are now very well organized, and the pallets with the stones are labeled: blue for those that are reusable or useful for faithfully rebuilding elements. Lise Leroux, engineer and specialist in the lab's "stone" department, shows me a piece that could belong to the wing of an angel. This job requires so much patience and rigor! These engineers and researchers are proper investigators.

Following two pages: Sculptural elements of the spire are preserved at the Cité de l'architecture et du patrimoine museum, as is the rooster that belongs at the top.

Entreprise Monduit / Monduit Company
L'AIGLE DE SAINT-JEAN L'ÉVANGÉLISTE
THE EAGLE OF SAINT JOHN THE EVANGELIST
D'après un modèle de / after a model by Adolphe Victor Geoffroy-Dechaume
1856-1861
Cuivre / Copper

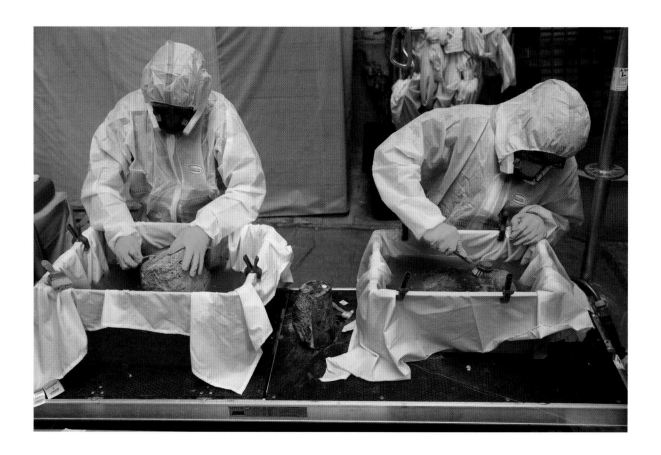

I am at the LRMH, located in Champs-sur-Marne, in the Seine-et-Marne department. I had asked its director, Aline Magnien, to let me know when the process to clean the stones saved from the fire would take place. Every stone previously stored

in the site's marquees is analyzed by architects and experts to determine which ones can be reused.

In Champs-sur-Marne, researchers from the Research Laboratory for Historical Monuments (LRMH) clean the stones from the cathedral.

The stones from Notre-Dame are cataloged, photographed, and analyzed. I observe these specialists who pay so much attention to these stones, and am really moved. I get the impression that when they photograph them, it is as if they were capturing the portrait of a person.

Sunday, September 13, 2020. This week, I went to Notre-Dame twice to photograph the dismantling operation of the large organ that began a few weeks ago. On Tuesday, the five organ builders present tackled the reed stops *en chamade;* that is, the small- and medium-sized horizontal pipes. I liked it and took a lot of pictures. One of them, Bertrand Cattiaux, has been looking after the organ of Notre-Dame for forty-eight years. Mario, the team leader, willingly engages in the photo shoot, posing without me even asking him.

Although the organ was not damaged by the flames or the water from the firefighters' hoses, lead dust has settled throughout the large instrument, and some parts have suffered from the differences in temperatures, notably during the heat wave in July 2019.

My favorite backdrop is that of the big organ and the atmosphere it creates. Behind the front, with its huge vertical and *en chamade* pipes, are hidden thousands of small pipes that are installed on two levels. You get to this section by going down one floor from the gallery, then up a small staircase that leads to a narrow corridor where you eventually discover all these pipes on your right. You get the feeling of being in the bowels of this gigantic musical machine. Or in the innards of an ocean liner. Everything is made of wood in this secret part, and it reminds me of what used to be called "the forest" of the cathedral before it went completely up in smoke.

Friday, October 30, 2020. Recently, I went to take photos of the cleaning and restoration test sites in two of the chapels, one located in the nave and the other, dedicated to Saint Ferdinand, in the choir. I was guided by the chief architect for historical monuments (ACMH), Pascal Prunet, who, together with Rémi Fromont, assists Philippe Villeneuve. To isolate them from the rest of the construction site, the chapels were kitted out with huge marquees into which air is constantly injected and then let out again, because the area is considered to be contaminated with lead. We had to wear respirator masks. The restorers have uncovered remnants of medieval murals.

In the Saint Ferdinand chapel, it took me several hours to capture three restorers in a very colorful setting. With all their gear, they looked like beekeepers.

I had not immediately noticed this head peeking through the scaffolding floor. I hurry to immortalize this rather funny detail.

I would learn later that this sculpture depicts Cardinal Morlot, the eighteenth archbishop of Paris.

It's been a while since I went to the choir of the cathedral. Craftspeople are at work there. I photograph the statues there, which have been wrapped in white drapes and look like ghosts.

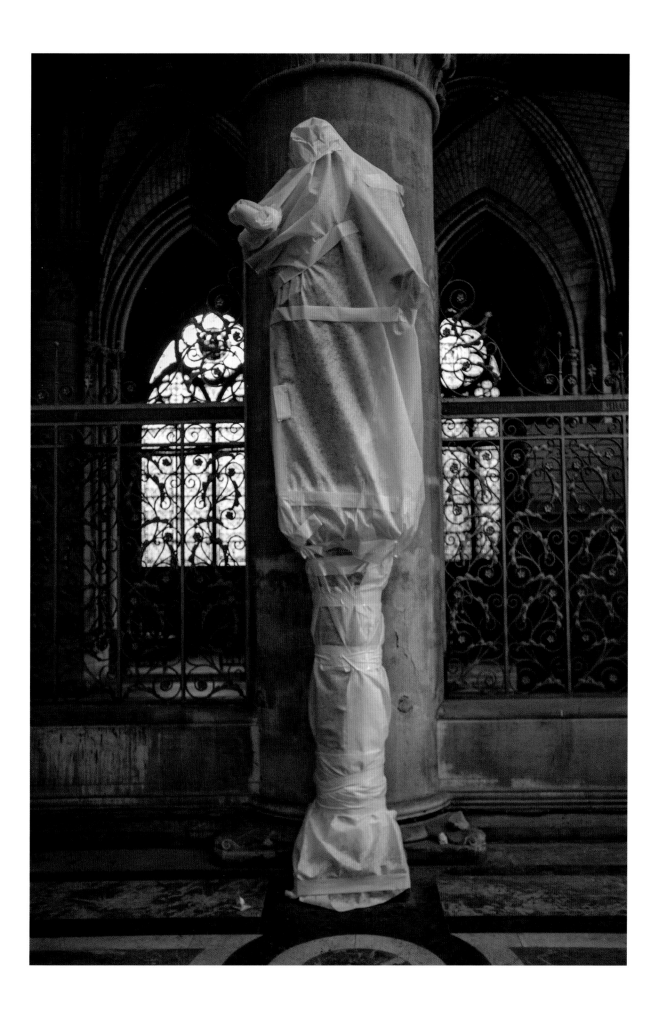

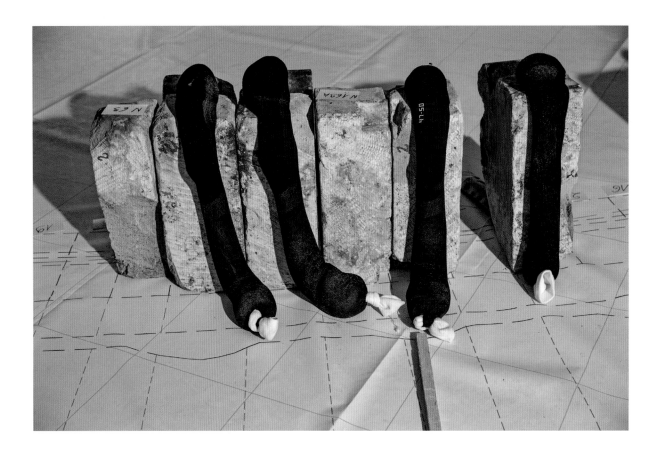

Friday, December 4, 2020. I have already been to Notre-Dame several times this week. I bumped into Pascal Prunet, one of the chief architects for historical monuments (ACMH), who tells me that a transverse arch in the nave–the only one that collapsed during the fire–will soon be reconstructed in the marquees. The nave has six double bays, and this transverse arch is the one that separates the penultimate from the last bay. Some of the stones at the base of the arch have withstood the fire, while those voussoir stones at the center, held in place

by the pressure, have collapsed. I talk to Frédérique Meyer, who grants me access. In the first step, the stones were identified as belonging to this arch, photographed, classified, and cleaned, before being placed meticulously at their place within the arch, but lying on the ground, in one of the marquees. Pascal Prunet inspects the reconstructed arch and answers questions from the teams, all while carefully analyzing each stone.

That same week, on another day, I witnessed the installation of the stained-glass windows that had been removed from the Saint Ferdinand chapel at the beginning of the restoration works.

Following pages. Top left: Chastity, thirteenth century, west rose window; **top right:** apostle (Saint Bartholomew), thirteenth century, south rose window; **bottom left:** crown-bearing angel, thirteenth century, south rose window; **bottom right:** Gregory VII, painted by Laurent-Charles Maréchal, known as Maréchal de Metz, 1861, south transept (picture window 304)

I make the acquaintance of Thierry Bruniou, a master glassmaker of Breton origin, as he tells me. He is very friendly.

I visit the stained-glass-restoration workshop of Emma Isingrini-Groult, master glassmaker. She gently passes a brush over the nose of a figure, who reminds me of a mythological hero, and removes layers of soot, lead, and dust, to reveal the original colors and make his face light up again.

This stained-glass window of Saint Denis is the work of the glass painter Charles Laurent Maréchal de Metz, 1859; high window in the choir (picture window 203).

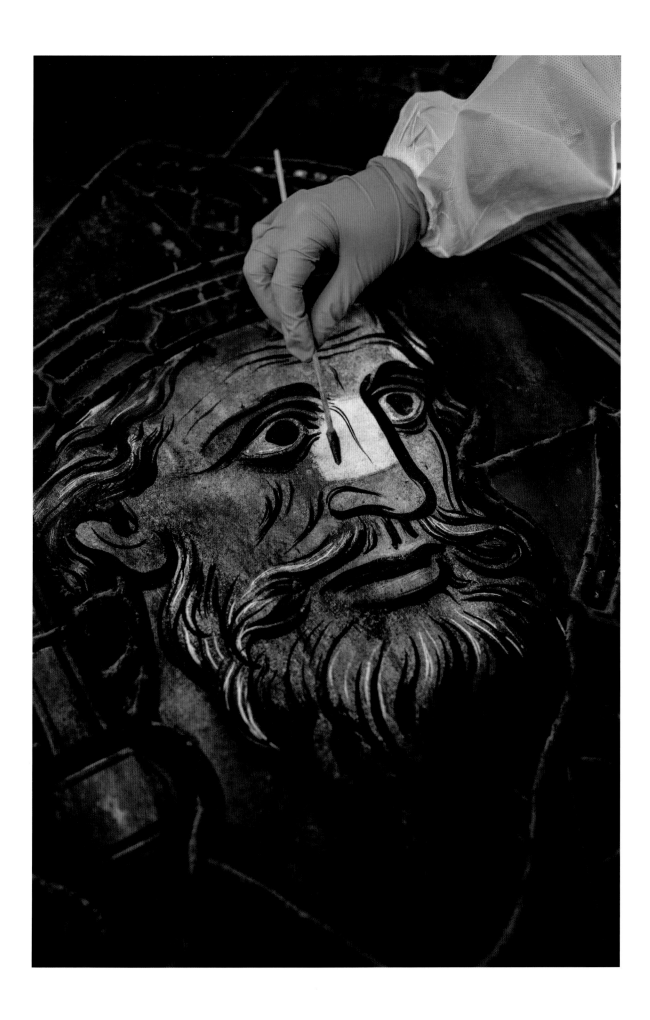

Heritage over the Centuries

T hanks to its doctrines, its impressive organization skills, and important building works, the nineteenth-century preserved buildings have been passed down to us, two hundred years later, without any damage other than accidental. But they could not have been handed down to us over the past two centuries if the art objects, stained-glass windows, furniture, statues, and organs, and the structure itself, had not already survived for six or even eight centuries.

Several documents already testify to a long-standing interest in Notre-Dame de Paris. First, several extracts on its history were written from the sixteenth century onward. In addition, many drawings and engravings from the ancien régime depict the empty cathedral without the pomp of a ceremony, which demonstrates people's interest in the building itself. On multiple occasions, models of the cathedral have been exhibited, and these can still be admired in the collections of the Carnavalet Museum and the Cité de l'architecture et du patrimoine. The remarkably close correspondence between these models and other representations of Notre-Dame prior to its restoration highlights how much care was taken to faithfully represent the cathedral.

In addition, building works were often undertaken with genuine conservation efforts in mind. In the eighteenth century, for example, the south rose window and the statues on the western façade were restored, and the vault of the transept crossing was rebuilt identically, although it could have been redesigned in a modern style. In contrast, the choir was rearranged at that time, which deserves further explanation. The recommendations of the Council of Trent could indeed have been the pretext for a rapid update of places of worship to reflect the liturgical adjustments. But it doesn't seem as if there was much eagerness to adopt the changes; on the contrary, it would take until 1699, a century and a half later, for the works to be actually undertaken. The medieval choir not only was preserved during this period but had in fact remained essentially the same since the thirteenth century; that is to say, five centuries earlier. This preservation over half a millennium—one could add, despite the (many) opportunities to remodel it—obviously reflects the interest in it, at least as a marker of tradition and rootedness. The displayed medieval sculptures as well as the large rose windows and many liturgical objects have also been preserved throughout the centuries.

Thus, the logic of preserving the legacy of the past and of passing it on to future generations existed long before the nineteenth century. In the eighteenth century, this approach was followed insofar as it did not hinder the functional use of the place. Thus, when in 1771 the architect Jacques-Germain Soufflot had the trumeau of the central portal demolished to facilitate processions, he took the necessary precautions to retain the upper part of the sculptures—although it would have been much easier to simply remove these. Several stained-glass windows were destroyed in 1752 to let more light into the interior, but the three large rose windows were preserved.

We might regret that the removals and destructions of the eighteenth century took place without leaving behind notes on what was removed. Yet, the nineteenth century proceeded in much the same way: neither the transept roof truss nor the disassembled south rose window was described for posterity. Let us have a closer look at the modifications made to the gallery vaults, which will allow us to match the building structure with its historical purpose rather than rereading history through the structure. We will have to wait for the restoration works to be complete to ascertain whether great cathedrals, such as Notre-Dame, should count as historical monuments, and thus whether the neo-Gothic and theories of the nineteenth century should play a part in its legacy. It is above all the image, even the imaginary picture of heritage, that we protect and not the heritage work itself, as suggested in Viollet-le-Duc's very famous definition of the term "restoration":

Restoring a building is not about maintaining, repairing, or remodeling it; it is about restoring it to a complete state that may never have existed at any given time.

The nineteenth-century restoration works also went hand in hand with the production of neo-Gothic goldworks, the most important of which is the reliquary of the crown of thorns. These are housed in the neo-Gothic sacristy at the side of the cathedral. The hegemony of this neo-Gothic style had reached its peak: the cathedral has become complete, from its history to its walls, from its annex buildings to the smallest of objects it contains, frozen in a fantastical imagination of the Middle Ages.

Toward the end of the nineteenth century, a gradual movement changed the cathedral: alternative forms emerged in the goldworks, and then in the 1930s, the figurative art deco stained-glass windows of the nave were created. They were produced after a long debate known as the "Stained-Glass Quarrel," during which the defenders of the neomedieval style opposed those in favor of contemporary art. The choice of these stained-glass windows, which were never installed due to the outbreak of World War II and were eventually replaced by stained-glass windows from the 1960s, marks a turning point for Notre-Dame de Paris, while the Second Vatican Council would give the cathedral a final touch of modernity.

After twenty years of reflection and trying out different configurations, construction eventually began to reconfigure the choir following the Second Vatican Council. The project was led by Cardinal

Lustiger, and the new altar was created by the sculptors Jean and Sébastien Touret. Several models were produced, set up, and tested at night.

It became one of the very first occasions on which the liturgical recommendations put forward by the council were put into practice in France. The bronze altar, designed for the concelebration in perfect communion with the congregation, is the most symbolic of its elements; it was crushed when the vault above the transept crossing collapsed on April 15, 2019. Whether you are receptive to religion or not, this altar was the embodiment of one of the greatest reforms of the Catholic Church, which did not affect merely the world of believers but constitutes one of the most important events in the history of the twentieth century. This perspective leads us to understand that the reason behind restoration works goes beyond the value of an object in the artistic sense.

The nineteenth century constantly sought to save what was under threat: the most-fragile elements affected by wear and tear over time, and the choices made by people. This approach made it possible for people of the nineteenth century to protect medieval churches from the point of view they set out to defend. In hindsight, we might be tempted to judge what this century has bequeathed to us, and to retain only what is of value in our modern-day eyes. But we do not have the liberty to agree or disagree with history. If we wanted to rewrite it, we would do precisely that for which we might reproach the nineteenth century; namely, to reconstruct a past on the basis of the perceptions of our time. On the contrary, we must pay tribute to the story of those who have defended heritage sites, and to what they have passed on to us, materially and intellectually. Aware of the biases of this heritage, we must enrich it, deepen what it explored, and open up new perspectives on heritage, especially in terms of its uses. We cannot in fact understand churches, with their unique floor plans not shared by any other type of building, without taking into account that what happens inside them has an impact on the building, its form, and its structure to its very core.

Recovering Notre-Dame:
December 2020–March 2021

Friday, December 4, 2020. I have already been to Notre-Dame several times this week. It took me a day to photograph the entire cathedral and in particular the transept crossing, once the scaffolding had been completely dismantled. I have to admit: seeing it like that was emotional.

The final steps of dismantling the
old scaffolding in the winter of 2020

It is as if the cathedral, full of holes, were
naked, once it had been rid of the thousands
of tubes that had imprisoned it. It felt like
rediscovering it. The gaping hole caused by
the fire made me think of a war photograph,
comparable to Dresden after it had been
bombed.

Wednesday, February 17, 2021. The access routes are changing quickly, to keep pace with the development of the site. A guy from the scaffolding company Europe Échafaudage accompanies me. We climb to the top of the scaffolding set up in the choir to allow for the installation of the centerings that will support the vault arches. From there, I photograph the rope access technicians tidying up the last chunks of debris left on top of the arches and vault, with the huge net spun across and the two towers behind them.

I finished the day at the top of the scaffolding set up in the choir. I hoped to find the craftspeople at work there this time. Luckily, there were quite a few of them. I spent a lot of time with the scaffolders and the AWP workers as they went up to secure the old scaffolding that had been engulfed by flames. I realize that these moments already belong to the past. They have all well and truly become "memories," as Pierron, one of the scaffolders, points out. My photos of this monster made up of thousands of tubes melted and folded upon itself have become historical documents since this scaffolding no longer exists.

Thursday, February 18, 2021. I was on-site yesterday, and it went very well. I started by walking across the frame floor of the transept crossing on the nave side. The timing was perfect. By the time the rope access technicians were setting up, around 2:00 p.m., I was ready. There were rope access technicians at each arch.

The rope access technicians are harnessed up to install the wooden roof truss to support the arches.

I catch up with carpenter Yves Macel, who directs the work of installing the semicircular-arch centerings. It's impressive work. The undertaking is magnificent, as is the view of the Pantheon.

I finish with a series of portraits of Yves, in particular, who is adorable and cooperative, despite the technical problems he has to solve.

Semicircular-arch centerings custom-made in Jarny, in the Meurthe-et-Moselle department, each weighing over a ton, are installed to secure the most-fragile arches of the cathedral's vaulted ceiling.

I find the rope access technicians again suspended from the springing of the southwest vault arches, like astronauts in space, ready for action.

The stones from the vaults that did not collapse during the fire are reattached by stonemasons, with the help of rope access technicians, using an ointment based on plaster and oakum that will soon have to be removed again for restoration.

Monday, March 29, 2021. You can no longer see the transept crossing for all the nets. I photograph some scaffolders, including my buddy Pierron.

We walk out onto the frame floor that dominates the hole. Three sections still need to be plastered with a mixture of plaster and oakum specially developed to secure them. The stonemasons and rope access technicians are getting ready. It's a spectacular sight.

The rope access technicians' operation
to secure the base of the ribs

I take portraits of Mathis and Arnaud, kitted out with helmets and full-face respirator masks while having various tools strapped over their hazmat suits.

Tuesday, April 20, 2021. I am on the side of the cathedral choir to document the supporting iron bars of an oculus being removed. This is where the centerings will pass through to support the vault arches of the nave. This oculus is located on the south face of the nave. These iron bars, which form something like a grid, have to be dismantled. They structure the stained-glass panels, which, although they were not affected by the flames, were removed in the days following the fire in order to be cleaned. They need to be restored because they are very worn and dirty. This process will take all morning. I play around composing images with the silhouettes of these balancing craftspeople looking like shadow puppets, in the spirit of Marc Riboud's photos on top of the Eiffel Tower. You can see the Pantheon at the back.

The craftspeople from Europe Échafaudage erect another structure on the north face of the crossing. It's always impressive to see them glide and rope-climb next to the void. This is one of the surprising aspects of this project: it is constantly moving. You go away one day and, a week later, return to discover a scaffolding is being erected, providing new access points and thus new perspectives. Everything happens very quickly.

Tuesday, March 9, 2021. Today is the day of a highly anticipated symbolic event: the felling of eight previously selected oaks in the Bercé national forest, near Le Mans. They will make up the straddle scaffold to rebuild the spire.

Frédérique Meyer has given me a description of the process, in which he details that these exceptionally large trees have been "selected from trees that have reached maturity and whose harvest has been planned to give way to a new generation. Managed by the National Forests Office (ONF), these oak trees have been grown in a high forest of trees of the same age, using a technique that has made it possible for over two hundred years to produce very slender trees."

The oaks are beautiful, majestic. To be among the lucky chosen ones, they must measure at least 656 feet (200 meters) in length and about 2.6 feet (80 centimeters) in average diameter. In total, a thousand trees will be used to rebuild the entire destroyed roof truss of the cathedral. The whole operation happens under the guidance and supervision of the National Forests Office and in close collaboration with the public body in charge, its architects, and experts. Frédérique tells me in his note that a first survey was carried out "in the presence of Rémi Fromont, who, in 2014, had designed a plan for the roof truss of the cathedral, and François Auger, heritage architect and carpenter and a member of the craftspeople guild Compagnons du Devoir, preselected sixteen oaks."

A first reconnaissance was carried out to initially select sixteen oaks with the help of Rémi Fromont. We were in the forest of Bercé in the Sarthe department, which was then covered with snow. It was beautiful but freezing!

Epilogue

Friday, June 11, 2021. I climbed to the top of the tower crane to photograph the cathedral without scaffolding, without any more nets, and after the transept crossing had been cleaned.

Every time I am up here, I am always superecstatic. The view of Notre-Dame and Paris is magnificent.

At my request, the young guy who accompanies me calls a manager over the walkie-talkie to the west frame floor of the transept crossing, and I get to witness the deployment of the "umbrella" that covers the hole. A set of white tarpaulins are spread across this wounded beauty, as if the cathedral were leaving an operating theater. Notre-Dame is indeed healing.

I reconnect with Christophe, the crane operator. We talk about everything and anything. I ask him if he is going on vacation: "Yes, probably to Corsica. That will do us good, my sweetheart and I. A nice change of skyscape." You can't make up such a slip of the tongue, from a crane operator who had just told me how lucky he was to experience Paris from up in the air!

An "umbrella" made of PVC tarpaulins and aluminum girders has been stretched over the transept crossing to prevent rainwater from damaging the cathedral choir.

THE AUTHORS

Patrick Zachmann has been a freelance photographer since 1976. He joined Magnum Photos agency in 1985 and became a member in 1990. The memory of people, of communities, or, more recently, of stones runs as a memorial red thread through his photographic work. His photographic essays reveal the complexity of the communities whose identity and culture he interrogates. In 1984, he produced a photographic work in the northern districts of Marseille with young people with migration backgrounds. Then, triggered by a personal project, he published his second book in 1987, *Enquête d'identité: Un Juif à la recherche de sa mémoire* (*Investigation of Identity: A Jew in Search of His Memory*). In 1989, his photographs of the events in Tiananmen Square in Beijing were widely disseminated in the international press. In 1990, he received the Niépce Prize.

Zachmann continued his study of the Chinese diaspora around the world for another six years, culminating in 1995 with the publication of *W. ou l'oeil d'un long-nez* (*W. or the Eye of a Long-Nose*) as well as an exhibition.

In 2016, Zachmann exhibited the entirety of his thirty years of work on China at the Maison Européenne de la Photographie and published *So Long, China* with Xavier Barral Publishing (Nadar Prize, 2016). In 2018–2019, he documented the new excavations of Pompeii.

After the fire of April 15, 2019, ravaged Notre-Dame de Paris, he undertook photographic work on the restoration of the building. In collaboration and partnership with the French Ministry of Culture, the public body responsible for the conservation and restoration of Notre-Dame, and Magnum Photos, his photographs taken in 2019 have already been the subject of two exhibitions on the fence running around the construction site. One looked back on the first two years on-site, while the other highlighted the professions and know-how involved to secure the building.

The Musée national d'Art et d'Histoire du Judaïsme dedicated a retrospective to him in December 2021.

Olivier de Châlus is an expert in all matters Notre-Dame de Paris. While he was a civil-engineering trainee, only a few steps away from the cathedral, the construction of the building already intrigued him. In 2008, he joined the team of cathedral tour guides, which he led from 2015 until the fire of 2019. In 2014, his reflections also led him to PhD studies at the University of Paris 1 Panthéon-Sorbonne, where he is currently completing his dissertation on Notre-Dame and the evolution of medieval construction techniques. Following the fire, he became the spokesperson for the association Scientifiques au service de la restauration de Notre-Dame de Paris (Scientists at the Service of the Restoration of Notre-Dame de Paris) and a member of the working group on stone and mortar of the scientific construction site, jointly led by the CNRS and the French Ministry of Culture, which backs the restoration site.

ACKNOWLEDGMENTS

I would like to thank the public body responsible for the conservation and restoration of the Notre-Dame Cathedral of Paris, which carries out the project management, and in particular the following:

General Jean-Louis Georgelin, special representative of the president of France and president of the public body responsible for the conservation and restoration of Notre-Dame; Jérémie Patrier-Leitus, director of communication, development, and cultural programming; Frédérique Meyer, press and media relations manager; and Brieuc Clerc, task officer.

My thanks also go to the French Ministry of Culture, to Cécile Ozanne, representative for information and communication, and to Barbara Pennamen, deputy representative; to the Directorate of Cultural Affairs (DRAC) Ile-de-France; and to Marie-Hélène Didier, head curator at the Commission on Historical Monuments.

To Philippe Villeneuve, Rémi Fromont, and Pascal Prunet, chief architects for historical monuments (ACMH).

To Didier Cuiset, director of Europe Échafaudage, and Franck Pagnussat, site supervisor; Didier Durand, CEO of Pierrenoël; Julien Le Bras, CEO of Le Bras Frères; Yves Macel, carpenter and head technician for installing the semicircular-arch centerings; and Xavier Rodriguez, CEO of Jarnias, and Guérin Chatenet, site supervisor.

I thank the scaffolders, the rope access technicians, the carpenters, the stonemasons, the aerial platform workers and crane operators, the iron craftspeople, the master glassmakers, the organ builders, the mural restorers, and the restorers of the stone and metal sculptures, as well as all the journey people and craftspeople who had the kindness and patience to let me be among them during the impressive operations to secure the cathedral, particularly Christophe Haroutounian and the master glassmakers Emma Isingrini-Groult and Thierry Bruniou. We must not forget the security guards, who often pointed out unsuspected vantage points to me.

For their scientific work, I would like to thank the following at the CNRS / French Ministry of Culture, along with the Research Laboratory for Historical Monuments (LRMH): Aline Magnien, director; Thierry Zimmer, deputy director; and Aurélia Azéma, Lise Leroux, Claudine Loisel, and Delphine Syvilay; at the French National Institute for Preventive Archaeological Research (INRAP): Marc Viré, study and research engineer; and at the French National Centre for Scientific Research (CNRS): Maxime L'Héritier, archeologist. Thanks also to Michel Hérold, head heritage curator, and Élisabeth Pillet from the André Chastel Center.

Thanks to the Magnum Paris team, especially Giulietta Palumbo for her precious help in the long run; to Clarisse Bourgeois for her rigor, her sharp eye, and her professional conscience that made her see beyond the reasonable; to Enrico Mochi, Naïma Kaddour, Sophie Marcilhacy, and Margot Becka; at Magnum London and New York, thanks to Bruno Bayley, Natalie Ivis, and Jade Chao; and to Christophe

Calais for his constant stimulation and for encouraging me to keep a diary. Thanks to Gaëlle Beaujean.

Thanks to Andrew Katz for his trust and loyalty, which have led to many beautiful publications in *Time* magazine, and to *Figaro Magazine*, *L'Obs*, *Le Monde*, *Libération*, *Télérama*, *Géo*, and *Stern*, and other publications that have featured my photographs and photo reportage.

I thank all the people who let themselves be photographed on-site and who have trusted in me, as well as the neighborhood residents who welcomed me to their homes, including Mr. and Mrs. Charensol, Maurice Desmazures, Patrice Lejeune, and Florence Mathieu. Also, all those I met at the "base camp" and on the construction site and whom I did not name here explicitly.

I also thank the team at Bayard Editions and especially Anne-Sophie Jouanneau, without whom this book would not exist, as well as Carole Schilling for her patience.

Finally, thank you to all my friends and family who have never stopped encouraging me with their enthusiasm.

Patrick Zachmann